National Museums Scotland

...Scotland

Frances and Gordon Jarvie

SCOTTIES SERIES EDITORS
Frances and Gordon Jarvie

Contents

...edition published in 2009

...MS Enterprises Limited – Publishing

...sion of NMSE Enterprises Limited

...nal Museums Scotland

...bers Street, Edinburgh EH1 1JF

© Frances and Gordon Jarvie 2009

...ges (for © see below and on page 40)

ISBN: 978-1-905267-24-8

Book design concept by Redpath.
Cover design by Mark Blackadder.
Layout by NMSE–Publishing.
Printed and bound in the United Kingdom by
Henry Ling Ltd, Dorchester, Dorset.

CREDITS

*Thanks are due to the following individuals and
organisations who have supplied images and
photographs for this publication.*

*Every attempt has been made to contact copy-
right holders to use the material in this publication.
If any image has been inadvertently missed, please
contact the publisher.*

NATIONAL MUSEUMS SCOTLAND
(© National Museums Scotland)

– for all cover images (including 609 Squadron
Spitfire 1A at RAF Drem airfield, 1940; Graf
Zeppelin LZ-127 over Musselburgh, 1932);
– and for pages 4 (Tytler); 6 (Lunardi); 7 ('Fowls');
8 (RAF badge, Barnwell Biplane); 9 (RFC pilot,
voucher, RNAS sign); 10 (propeller); 11 (propeller,
Lanark memorabilia); 12-13 (all R34 photographs); 14 (poster); 15 (*Seafarer*); 16 (Spitfire,
Hawker Harts); 17 (603 Squadron booklet, Heinkel); 18 (Tiger Moth); 19 (gun ammo, War-time

photographs); 20 (propeller, Catalina, Blackburn
Perth flying boats); 21 (bomb, Supermarine S.6B);
22 (nuclear mask, secret bunker); 23 (RAF Missile
Launcher, Avro Vulcan); 24 (Eurofighter jet, Loganair Islander); 26 (S.A.L. badge, Bulldog trainer);
27 (Timeline photographs); 28 (Percy Pilcher with
Hawk); 29 (*Scottish Flyer* magazines, balloon); 30
(Weir's autogyros); 32 (stewardess, aeroplane);
33 (all photographs); 34 (engine, Concorde); 35
(Concorde in hangar, flight deck); 37 (Gemini
space capsule); 40 (National Museum of Flight)

FURTHER CREDITS ON PAGE 40.

SCOTTIE BOOKS

**For a full listing of NMS Enterprises
Limited – Publishing titles and related
merchandise:**

www.nms.ac.uk/books

Stuff of dreams
Father John Damian

It was the stuff of dreams for mankind to be able to fly. Ever since the Greek hero Icarus flew too near the sun, which melted the wax holding the feathers in his wings together, brilliant minds have been at work on the challenge of flight.

The story of Icarus was a Greek legend.

In the late 1400s the Italian artist Leonardo da Vinci drew amazing flying machines. But it was to be centuries later that the real conquest of the skies began.

In the reign of King James IV of Scotland many momentous discoveries and inventions were made. The Atlantic Ocean, for example, began to replace the Mediterranean Sea as the world's highway. In 1492 an explorer called Christopher Columbus 'discovered' America. By 1498 another explorer, Vasco da Gama, reached India via the Cape of Good Hope. Then, twenty years later, Ferdinand Magellan made the first sea voyage around the world.

?
Quick question
What parts of the world were *not* known to people who lived in Europe five hundred years ago?

Answer on page 39

King James IV (1473-1513) and his Queen, Margaret Tudor, daughter of Henry VII of England.

In Scotland at this time James IV wanted to better people's lives. He founded a new university at Aberdeen (Scotland's third), and ordered landowners to send their eldest sons to school at age eight – chiefly to learn Latin and law. Many ships were built to protect the merchant fleet and the king was known as the 'Founder of the Scottish Navy'. James IV could speak many languages and he always liked to meet and talk with clever people who could teach him something new.

It was an Italian friar, John Damian, who came to the king and boasted that he knew how to fly. Unwisely, Damian had also claimed that he could make gold out of lead. When his efforts were in vain, he tried to impress by flying off the castle wall at Stirling. As a result, he fell into a midden and broke his leg. And what was Father Damian's lame excuse? 'There were *hen* feathers in the wings!' Hens are not noted for their flying skills!

Leonardo da Vinci

The Italian artist and inventor Leonardo da Vinci (1452-1519) spent hours studying the flight of bats and birds, carefully examining their wing structure and the resistance of the wings to the air. He devised a flapping wing machine, as well as ideas for a helicopter and parachute. His drawings are technically brilliant.

Stirling Castle, between 1890 and 1900.

Balloon mania
James Tytler (1745-1804)

The period 1770 to 1830 was known as the Age of Enlightenment or the Golden Age in Scotland. Improvements were being made to people's lives beyond their wildest imagination.

'Balloon Tytler', born in Angus, was a brilliant man who sadly spent most of his life in poverty.

An admission ticket, signed by James Tytler himself, to view his balloon.

There was a huge leap forward from the dark days of medieval times to a much brighter future. The Scots inventor James Watt, for example, perfected the steam engine. The architect James Craig won a competition to design the New Town of Edinburgh. The economist Adam Smith wrote *The Wealth of Nations* about free trade; while David Hume became a great philosopher or thinker.

James Tytler, known as 'Balloon Tytler', was the first known Scottish aviator. This multi-talented man served as a ship's surgeon on a whaler, then worked as a chemist and journalist. In 1784 he rose 107 metres in a hot-air balloon, the first person in the United Kingdom to do so. The ten-minute journey in Edinburgh took him from Abbeyhill to Restalrig, although it ended suddenly when he had to throw out the stove while the balloon ascended.

Tytler's home-made balloon followed the example set by the Montgolfier brothers in France. But his genius as a pioneer aviator was overlooked. His work as editor of the *Encyclopedia Britannica* was his lasting legacy. This was a painstaking task, but a huge achievement.

⚒ How does it work?

A hot-air balloon is like a huge bag of lighter-than-air gas. Lift is created by heating the air inside the balloon. To descend, hot air is let out through a vent. It is the cooler heavier air that makes the balloon drop in height.

Below: The balloon launched by the Montgolfier brothers in 1783, ascending from the Palace of Versailles, France, in the presence of the royal family.

The Montgolfier brothers

Joseph-Michel and Jacques-Étienne Montgolfier were sons of a paper manufacturer in France. In 1782 they created a hot-air balloon which travelled six miles across Paris, the first manned flight in an untethered craft. However, their experiments came to a halt because of the French Revolution. Tytler would probably have read about their work in newspapers in the Edinburgh coffee houses.

No one in those days recognised that James Tytler was an important pathfinder in Scottish flight. However, there was an Italian balloonist who had heard of his exploits – a Vincenzo Lunardi from Lucca in Tuscany. More about him on the next page ….

Lunardi from Lucca
Vincenzo Lunardi (1759-1806)

'Hear Ye! Hear Ye! … Vincent Lunardi will make an ascent in his balloon from the green of Heriot's Hospital at half-past two today … Hear Ye! Hear Ye!'

Lunardi visited Edinburgh in 1785, the year after Tytler's balloon ascent. In October 1785 he made his own daring ascent from Heriot's Hospital green (now George Heriot's School). The event drew lots of attention. Shops were shut and businesses ground to a halt. At least 80,000 people gathered to gawp in sheer amazement.

'At 12 o'clock a flag was displayed from the Castle and a gun was fired from the green when the process of filling the balloon began. At half-past two it was completely inflated.' Lunardi soared 'like a sky rocket', waving his flag over the city.

He then flew close to the island of Inchkeith, before going east to North Berwick. Finally, at the mercy of the winds, he flew over to Fife near Ceres. Before landing he sounded a trumpet – much to the alarm of the local farm workers.

Vincent Lunardi standing in the basket of his hydrogen-filled balloon.

Lunardi had achieved nearly three miles in height, endured snow, and had almost pitched into the sea before throwing out some ballast to save himself. The Ceres church bell rang to welcome him and he was hailed as a hero in nearby Cupar. Next day, the Club of Gentlemen Golfers in St Andrews also honoured him.

There were further ascents in the Borders, from Glasgow ('his ascent was very majestic'), and Edinburgh again. After the second ascent from Heriot's Hospital the basket landed in the Forth. Luckily Lunardi had a cork jacket 'in case of an immersion in the German ocean' (the North Sea).

Fashion statement

Scottish lady admirers of Lunardi wore bonnets shaped like a balloon. This fashion craze led the famous Scottish poet Robert Burns to write 'The Address to a Louse', a poem about a beastie crawling over a Lunardi bonnet.

Complaining to the louse, Burns writes:

… I wadna been surprised to spy
You on an auld wife's flannen toy;[1]
Or aiblins some bit duddie boy,
On's wyliecoat;[2]
But Miss's fine Lunardi! – fie!
How daur ye do't?

[1] flannel hat [2] flannel waistcoat

Fowls of a Feather Flock together

VINCENZO LUNARDI

BORN IN LUCCA, ITALY, IN 1759, HE ASCENDED IN A HYDROGEN BALLOON ON 5TH OCTOBER 1785 FROM THE GARDEN OF HERIOT'S HOSPITAL, EDINBURGH. HE LANDED AT COALTOWN OF CALLANGE IN THE PARISH OF CERES, HAVING TRAVELLED 46 MILES. THIS WAS THE FIRST AERIAL VOYAGE IN SCOTLAND.

Above: Lunardi's memorial plaque near Ceres in Fife.

Left: James Tytler (left of centre) about to shake hands with Lunardi (centre).

Fast fact

Today more than 100,000 Scots can trace their ancestry to Italy, the land of Lunardi's birth. Glasgow has more Italian restaurants per square mile than anywhere else in the United Kingdom.

Plot the course

Draw a map outline of the Firth of Forth. Mark the course of Lunardi's balloon trip from Edinburgh to Ceres. (You can still see the exact landing place marked in a corner of a field on the road between Ceres and Cupar – see the plaque above.)

First World War
Airpower, the new weapon of war

On 28 June 1914 Austrian Archduke Franz Ferdinand was assassinated in Sarajevo, the capital of Bosnia and Herzegovina – a spark that ignited a catastrophic world war.

Back in 1895, however, the daring Percy Pilcher flew his fragile *Bat* glider from a farm near Cardross (see page 28). Then, in 1909, the Barnwell brothers made short flights near Stirling in a plane of their own design – the first powered flights in Scotland. Frank Barnwell (1880-1938) went on to become the chief designer of the Bristol Aeroplane Company. Known as Britain's answer to the famous American Wright brothers, tragically both Barnwell brothers died in separate flying accidents.

In 1914 aircraft were set to play an important role high above the battle-fields of a world at war. A typical British aircraft of this time had a top speed of 72 miles per hour and could be airborne for up to three hours. It was important that aircraft were easy to fly, as pilots only had a few hours of flight training! Planes were used as 'eyes in the sky' to find enemy positions in trench warfare.

Above: A badge of RAF East Fortune.
Below: The Barnwell Biplane in 1909.

Drawing of a First World War Royal Flying Corps pilot. Seated in open cockpits, pilots and navigators were exposed to extreme cold.

By 1918 planes were faster, more robust, and used for bombing, ground attack and naval warfare. Modern battle tactics had come of age.

At the outbreak of the First World War the main military airfield in Scotland was at Montrose, set up by the Royal Flying Corps (RFC) in 1913.

The Royal Naval Air Service (RNAS) also set up flying-boat and seaplane stations from Shetland in the north, East Fortune in the east, and Inchinnan, Glasgow, to the west. Both Edinburgh and Glasgow were under protection from the latter two stations which were also airship bases.

The first aircraft carriers in the world were based at Rosyth in Fife. There were many daring trials of aircraft landing on warships in the sheltered waters of the Forth. The Scottish-built Beardmore WBIII was the first type of Royal Navy aircraft designed for flight from an aircraft carrier. It had folding wings for easier storage. The Royal Navy's fleet at Rosyth was a prize target for German airships.

On 1 April 1918 the RFC and RNAS merged to become the Royal Air Force (RAF).

Tickets please?

After the War there were lots of surplus aircraft, so regular air routes were set up by Midland and Scottish Air Ferries as part of a new transport network. But it was to be a long time before budget fares arrived!

Montrose Air Station Heritage Centre

New squadrons left Montrose in 1916 to fight in France. Life expectancy for new pilots was just two weeks. The former airfield is said to be haunted by the souls of many downed pilots. It is said that sometimes a ghostly biplane can still be spotted in the air!

ROYAL NAVAL AIR STATION.

Be a flight detective

WWI airfields were often just a dirt runway, or flat field, with a few barns as hangars. Are there any signs of old airfields near you? If so, can you find out what kind of aircraft were flown there?

9

The first non-stop transatlantic flight

Sir Arthur Whitten Brown (1886-1948)

Born in Glasgow, Arthur Whitten Brown began his career in engineering. After being shot down, wounded and imprisoned in Germany during the First World War, he decided to use his aerial navigation skills on his return to Britain.

First World War propeller.

Arthur Whitten Brown became a lieutenant in the RAF and offered to navigate on the first non-stop transatlantic flight. John Alcock had already been chosen as the pilot. The flight was from St John's, Newfoundland in Canada, to Clifden, Connemara in Ireland. The west-to-east crossing was thought to be easier due to the benefit of the westerly winds.

The flight ended successfully on 15 June 1919, having covered 1980 miles in 16 hours 12 minutes. They used a Vickers Vimy aircraft for the flight, which only just had the range to complete the journey. (The Vimy was originally designed as a bomber during the First World War.) The two intrepid aviators won a prize of £10,000 which had been offered by the *Daily Mail* newspaper back in 1913.

Sadly, only a few months later John Alcock was killed in a flying accident. Arthur Whitten Brown never flew again, but he had navigated a true course despite all the difficulties … read on.

Fast fact

Alcock and Brown took a toy black cat called Twinkletoes with them on their journey! This statue of the famous pair stands outside the Heathrow Airport visitor centre.

Trials en route

1. The pilot-to-navigator wireless system used by Alcock and Brown broke down after take-off. They had to bellow at one another to be heard.

2. The electric heating in their flying suits broke down.

3. Alcock's goggles had to be de-misted by Brown – the pilot couldn't let go of the controls.

4. The exhaust pipe melted on one of the engines. It became so noisy that Alcock and Brown could no longer shout at one another and they now had to write notes.

5. They hit a storm in the middle of the night and nearly ditched into the sea.

Propeller commemorating the first Air Mail flight in the United Kingdom, 1911.

6. Brown could only set a true course if he saw the sun or the stars. It was bitterly cold above the clouds.

7. Early on 15 June the engines began to splutter: the air-intakes were seizing up. Brown crawled out on to the wings and cleared the ice with a pen-knife, a feat he performed five more times during the night.

8. The aviators finally landed safely in a bog. The soft ground probably saved their lives.

Imagine that you are Arthur Whitten Brown. As navigator, write the flight log of an hour's events in mid-Atlantic.

SCOTTISH INTERNATIONAL AVIATION MEETING.

6, 8th to 13th AUGUST 1910 LANARK

ON THE WEST COAST ROUTE
BETWEEN
ENGLAND AND SCOTLAND

Special Express Train Service between Glasgow (Central) Edinburgh (Princes Street) and Aviation Station adjoin...

CODY IN FLIGHT

Lanark 1910

200,000 visitors attended the 1910 Aviation Meeting at Lanark organised by the Scottish Aeronautical Society. There were 19 competitors flying in 13 different types of aeroplanes. All the entrants and the organisers were presented with a medal.

11

Monster of the air
The R34 airship

An airship is a self-powered, lighter-than-air craft, steered by rudders.

German Zeppelin airships made a terrifying raid on Edinburgh and Leith during the First World War, killing eleven people. Dozens of bombs rained down on the city. Pilots at Turnhouse Aerodrome formed Reserve Squadrons in 1916 to defend the city against these monsters of the air.

From the First World War new ways of travelling by air began to emerge – the aeroplane and the airship. In 1919 the R34 airship was built by the engineering factory of William Beardmore, Glasgow. It was not designed to carry passengers; indeed food had to be cooked on a plate welded to the engine exhaust pipe!

R34 leaving East Fortune on its transatlantic flight on the morning of 2 July 1919.

However, breaking records was the order of the day and the R34 was made ready for the first return Atlantic crossing.

Only two weeks after Alcock and Brown's successful flight, the R34 left East Fortune airfield in East Lothian, with eight officers, 22 crew, a stowaway and even a cat on board! Major George Scott from Dunbar was in charge of the crew.

Fighting strong head winds, a thunderstorm over Canada and freezing cold, the R34 reached Long Island in the United States in $4\frac{1}{2}$ days. An officer, Major Pritchard, parachuted to the ground to help anchor the craft, becoming the first person to arrive in America from Europe by air! The return journey was equally cold, but much faster (only 75 hours). The R34 landed safely at Pulham in Norfolk on 13 July at 6.57 am (GMT).

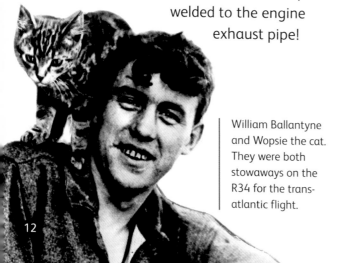

William Ballantyne and Wopsie the cat. They were both stowaways on the R34 for the transatlantic flight.

Airship versus aeroplane?

Airships required vast sheds for storage. It took large teams to help with landing and maintenance. As they were at the mercy of the wind, airships were very costly to run. A huge volume of gas was needed just to lift the craft.

Airships were also very dangerous. Filled with highly inflammable hydrogen, there was always a great risk of fire. The R34 crew was encouraged to sing or whistle while they worked. If their tone changed, it meant that gas was leaking!

Many people at the time thought that airships were going to replace the great ocean liners as a means of luxurious travel. However, the R101, built by the British Air Ministry for use on Empire routes, crashed in France in 1930 with the loss of 54 lives. It was the last airship to be built in Britain.

Airships finally lost out to aeroplanes in 1937 when the giant Zeppelin airship, the *Hindenburg*, burst into a massive fireball on landing near New York.

Website watch

www.vidicom-tv.com/hindenburg

Make up your own newspaper front page about the disaster of this 'Titanic of the Sky'.

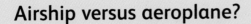

Right: The bow plate of the R34.

Background: The R34 airship in front of its hangar (with airship NS7 in the sky) at East Fortune in 1919.

Breaking records
1930s aviation 'firsts'

Poster referring to the first east–west crossing of the South Atlantic by Scottish pilot Jim Mollison.

From 'flying sweethearts' to real 'high flyers', rocket post to radar success, read on to find out more about some of Scotland's aviation 'firsts' in the 1930s.

James Mollison (1905-59) was a pioneer pilot from Glasgow who set many records during the 1930s. In 1931 he flew from Australia to Britain in 8 days 19 hours. In 1932 he set a record of 4 days 17 hours for flying from the United Kingdom to South Africa. During one flight he was matched with the English-born pilot

Amy Johnston, proposing marriage only eight hours after meeting her, and while still in the air! They became known as 'the flying sweethearts'.

'Winnie' Drinkwater of Midland and Scottish Air Ferries was Scotland's first female airline pilot – one of the few who made her mark in the 1930s.

Lord Clydesdale (who was later the **Duke of Hamilton**) was the chief pilot for the Houston Mount Everest Expedition in 1933. Accompanied by **Flight Lieutenant David McIntyre** they flew over the highest point on earth. Although they barely scraped over the mountain, battling fierce winds and freezing temperatures in an open cockpit, their two-seater Westland plane was thought 'fit for purpose' at the time. It was developed by the RAF and had a new engine which could fly at record heights.

Rocket post

In 1934 Gerhard Zucker experimented with rocket-delivered mail in the Western Isles. He fired the rocket over 1600 metres of water between Harris and the Isle of Scarp. Nervous officials watched as the rocket exploded, blowing the post all over the beach! The rocket contained 1200 pre-sold rocket postal covers and the singed envelopes were highly prized by collectors! Later, as Zucker was found to be a 'threat' to the Post Office and the country's security, he was deported back to his homeland of Germany.

A picture taken of the south face and summit of Mount Everest from one of the Westland biplanes used in the 1933 Houston Mount Everest Expedition, by Colonel Stewart Blacker.

The same Duke of Hamilton received a surprise guest in 1941. On the eve of Germany's attack on Russia, Adolf Hitler's deputy, Rudolph Hess, flew to Scotland to make peace between Germany and Britain so that together they could fight Russia. Having parachuted safely out of his Messerschmitt, he informed a shocked farmer, 'I have an important message for the Duke of Hamilton'.

On 22nd July 1933 Jim Mollison and his wife Amy Johnson attempted to fly across the Atlantic in a de Havilland Dragon, *Seafarer*. Their mission was sadly unsuccessful. (This plane is a similar example from the National Museums Scotland collections.)

Radar

Sir Robert Watson-Watt (1892-1973), from Brechin in Angus, was from the same family as James Watt, the 18th-century pioneer of the steam engine.

During the First World War, Watson-Watt worked as a weather expert for the RAF at Farnborough. From 1917 his work at the Meteorological Office (Met Office) was to design devices to locate thunder-storms. Later, in 1935, as head of radio research, he finished the project that was to win the Battle of Britain and eventually the Second World War – **radar**. Radar enabled enemy aircraft to be detected at any time and in any weather, although its success was often due to the patient operators of the WAAF (Women's Auxiliary Air Force).

Today, radar's legacy includes air traffic control systems around the world tracking every flight in the sky, as well as roadside speed cameras.

15

Second World War
Dogfights around the Firth of Forth

About 120,000 aircraft were built in Britain in the Second World War, almost 2000 in 1940 during the Battle of Britain.

Above: A Submarine 509 Spitfire T9 aircraft.

Below: A formation of Hawker Harts from 603 Squadron over the Forth Railway Bridge.

About 1.75 million people took part in aircraft production as the slow biplanes of the First World War were replaced by sleek monoplanes like the Spitfire.

Spitfires entered the war from Drem and Turnhouse in October 1939. Royal Navy warships at Rosyth came under attack from two waves of German bombers – Hitler's first raid over mainland Britain. The Auxiliary Squadrons of 602 (City of Glasgow) and 603 (City of Edinburgh) were scrambled to protect the Forth Railway Bridge and destroyers in the Forth.

Fierce dogfights led to two Junkers being shot down. A train on the bridge had a grandstand view of the action. Luckily, at that time the Germans honoured the code not to bomb civilian targets, but within weeks the bridge was protected by barrage balloons, floating above the structure like giant inflatable whales.

After this attack the RAF opened many bases around the Forth. People suffering from tuberculosis were being treated at that time at East Fortune (now the National Museum of Flight). They were evacuated to Bangour Hospital and the RAF fighter base at East Fortune was expanded.

Grangemouth Aerodrome was home to such aircraft as Blenheims, Defiants, Gladiators, Lysanders, Spitfires and Whirlwinds. By 1941 young pilots from Czechoslovakia, the Netherlands, Poland, America, and the Commonwealth, were being trained to win the war in the air.

Website watch

www.ww2inthehighlands.co.uk

This website has been designed by Cauldeen Primary School, Inverness. Find out about the air war in the Highlands and Islands.

- First, enter the site. Go to **Environmental Impact – Plane Crashes** and the crash of the **Sunderland W4026**. Find out why the aircraft was going to Iceland?

- Read the other stories from **Gairloch**, **Helmsdale**, **Lewis**, **Loch Ness** and **The Tragedy in the Moray Firth**.

- Go back to the main menu for **Local Memoirs**. Look at the photographs of **Flight Commander, 281 Squadron** from Evanton. How many different planes are shown and what types are they?

- Go to the **War Memorial** section under **Environmental Impact**. What is commemorated at the Aircrew Memorial Bandstand, Inverness?

- Also under **Environmental Impact**, look out for the **Skitten Memorial** near Wick. Read the story of **Operation Freshman**. Why was this such a dangerous, but vital, mission?

Below: A Heinkel HE-111 KG26 shot down by 602 and 603 squadron pilots at Humbie, near Edinburgh, in 1939. It was the first enemy aircraft to fall on the British mainland.

Right: 603 City of Edinburgh Squadron booklet (note the Forth Railway Bridge in the background).

Second World War
Airfields and air stations

Scottish airfields during the Second World War offered a complex network of training and operational needs. Each had an essential role.

The Avro Lancaster was the best known of the Second World War night bombers.

Squadrons on the Ayrshire and Fife coasts were used for anti-shipping patrols and missions. Fighter squadrons on the east coast – at Wick, Dyce, Peterhead, Montrose, Leuchars, Drem, East Fortune, Kinloss and Grangemouth – were used to defend the fleet at Rosyth and Scapa Flow. These major airfields were Coastal Command bases. The Royal Navy trained its own pilots for the Fleet Air Arm. Minor airfields dotted the country, and seaplane bases were situated in sheltered waters.

At HMS Jackdaw, Crail, it was Swordfish (nicknamed 'Stringbags') and Barracuda aircraft which roared down the run-ways. Crail was used as a torpedo school and trained pilots for night flying. Old destroyers and ferries were berthed in the Forth for torpedo practice. The odd dummy torpedo (one ton in weight) just missed a Royal Navy crew! At night Crail was protected by a decoy airfield (known as a Q site), lit up to copy the layout of the real airfield.

This Tiger Moth aeroplane was built for the RAF in 1940, and is the most famous training aircraft.

Fast fact

Crews from RAF Wick were well known to lighthouse-keepers in Orkney as they dropped newspapers to the isolated men ....

Across the Forth at East Fortune the RAF base was used for operational units to train nightfighter crews in planes like the Blenheim and Defiant. The first crews to be trained were from Australia, Canada, New Zealand and Poland. In 1942 East Fortune was transferred to Coastal Command and trained crews for anti-shipping strikes in Bristol Beaufighters. During the rest of the war East Fortune was used occasionally as a diversion airfield for Halifax and Lancaster bombers returning from operations over Germany.

By the war's end there were 94 military airfields in Scotland. Each had adapted to changing needs and new technologies, but many brave pilots never made it home again. In both world wars the RAF suffered more casualties in training and accidents than it did in operations.

Belt of machine-gun ammunition.

Website watch

Look up **Royal Naval Air Stations** on **wikipedia**

- Look at the list of Royal Naval Air Stations in use by different squadrons in Scotland.

- How many 'HMS' names have the name of a bird?

JACKDAW

- List the place and the name of the base: eg. RNAS Culdross (HMS Seahawk) or RNAS Crail (HMS Jackdaw).

- Choose one station nearest to your home. Design a station badge using the bird. (You may need a bird book with illustrations to help you.)

War-time work

Above: A de Havilland Mosquito kept at East Fortune RAF base.

Right: Polish air squadron based at Benbecula in the winter of 1944-45.

Above: Workers from the Women's Auxiliary Air Force at Turnhouse Aerodrome in 1944.

Flying boats and seaplanes

Flying boat propeller.

What's the difference?

A **flying boat** is like a boat with wings. Its hull is adapted for floating, yet is strong enough to ride a rough sea. These planes had a long range. In the Second World War the Sunderland carried a crew of ten and could stay in the air for up to 16 hours.

Above: A Catalina flying boat in Oban harbour, 1942.

Below: A model of a Blackburn Perth flying boat, the largest craft ever to serve with the RAF.

A **seaplane** is also designed to take off and land on water, but has two long floats instead of wheels. It can only land in calmer waters and has a shorter range.

RAF flying boats, such as Catalinas, Lerwicks and Sunderlands, protected our precious cargo boats during the Second World War. These lumbering aircraft were ideal for anti-submarine patrols and for forward air reconnaissance over the Atlantic.

Around the Scottish coast was a web of flying-boat bases from Stranraer in the south-west, to Islay, Rhu, Oban Bay, Kirkwall, Easter Ross and Dundee in the east. The Catalinas at Dundee took part in Special Operations and often flew agents into, and out of, Norway.

Scotland's first commercial seaplane service

Not far from where Sutherland flying boats were originally built in Dumbarton, you will find Loch Lomond Seaplanes. Today this service lets visitors view the National Park around Loch Lomond in an environmentally-friendly way.

Their Cessna Turbo Stationair makes visits to Scotland's coastline and inland lochs. The company has extended the service from the River Clyde to Oban and Mull – the first seaplane service in Europe to take off from a city centre.

Fast fact

As recently as October 2006, four unexploded bombs were found near the A9 in Easter Ross – at Catalina Junction (named after the RAF flying-boat base on the Cromarty Firth).

RAF target indicator bomb.

Learn to fly seaplanes!

You can learn to fly seaplanes at Loch Earn, Scotland's National Watersports Centre. Seaplanes can land on any stretch of water in Scotland (apart from reservoirs). In contrast, in England the law states that a plane must get permission to land on stretches of water.

Supermarine S.6B (forerunner of the Spitfire) was the outright winner of the Schneider Trophy in 1931, a prize competition for seaplanes that was first held in 1913.

Defence in the Cold War
The Royal Observer Corps

After the Second World War came the dark days of the four-minute warning. The world was poised on the brink of a full-scale nuclear war ....

No one knew exactly what was to be done in those four minutes, but the guardians of the nation (civil servants, military and government leaders) had their war rooms and secret bunkers. They were ready to issue further orders if there was anyone left to listen after a nuclear attack.

The Cold War was the result of the on-going distrust between the West and the Communist Soviet Bloc, with constant bluff and counter-bluff about the power of the nuclear weapons on each side. 'Nuclear winter' was a threat that every-one lived under – the fear of life on earth being blotted out.

Scotland's Secret Bunker, near Anstruther, was a closely guarded secret. It started as

Above: New equipment had to be designed to protect soldiers from the Nuclear, Biological and Chemical threats of the Cold War.

Below: A nuclear bunker built in 1965 at Kirk-newton near Edinburgh, complete with offices, sleeping quarters and fitted kitchens.

one of a chain of radar stations run by the RAF around the coastline just after the Second World War. It was designed to spot approaching Russian bombers and to direct fighter planes to intercept them.

Royal Observer Corps (ROC)

The ROC had a network of 336 underground monitoring posts in Scotland. Most were small reinforced concrete boxes, the size of a caravan, cold and very damp. The three-man ROC posts were designed to monitor nuclear bombs and the resulting fallout.

☢ The leftovers

The Cold War officially ended when the Berlin Wall was torn down in 1989. Most of the ROC posts were left to rot, padlocked and forgotten. Usually all that remains is a concrete hatchway above ground and a ventilation shaft.

(Please note: 23 Post at Skelmorlie in Ayrshire is open by arrangement.)

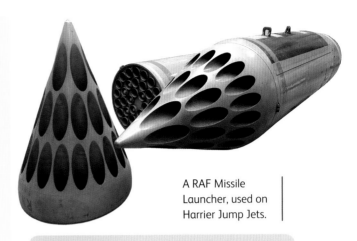

A RAF Missile Launcher, used on Harrier Jump Jets.

The war had left Scotland with a web of military airfields. Few were of use for the new nuclear age. Primary V-bomber bases were at Prestwick, Kinloss, Machrihanish, Leuchars and Lossiemouth. Secondary bases were at Dounreay and Wick. Dounreay was one of the 52 prime Soviet nuclear targets until at least 1990.

The RAF commissioned the famous V-bomber force – the Valiant, Victor and Vulcan models. They came into service between 1955 and 1958. Although able to fly to Moscow without refuelling, they needed a long concrete runway, at least one mile in length.

An Avro Vulcan bomber, built in 1963, with Blue Steel nuclear missile.

☢ Scotland's Secret Bunker

The Bunker is 40 metres in depth, with a shell of three-metre-solid concrete, built to withstand nuclear attack. It remained in use until 1992 and was opened as a museum in 1994. However, it is still so well hidden from view that many tourists go round in circles looking for it!

🏷 Website watch

www.bbc.co.uk/scotlandonfilm

Select **film and radio clips, work** and then **miscellaneous** to find **Joe Urban** who worked at the Secret Bunker when it was in operation.

Highlands and Islands airports

The largest and most frequently used Low Flying Area in the United Kingdom is the north-west Highlands.

A Eurofighter EF-2000 Typhoon F2 aircraft in full flight!

The Low Flying Area (LFA) of the North West Highlands, Western Isles, Orkney and Shetlands, is for operational low flying by RAF fast jets. Here planes can fly as low as 30 metres, which is very scary if you are on a hill in the middle of nowhere and a jet suddenly roars past *below* you!

A Loganair Islander aircraft, 1994, used as part of the vital Scottish ambulance service to remote communities.

?
Quick questions

Airports in the Highlands and Islands of Scotland have many unique features. Can you find at least three things about these airports which are unique to (a) Scotland, (b) Europe and (c) the World?

Answers on page 39

SCOTTISH AMBULANCE SERVICE

Airports

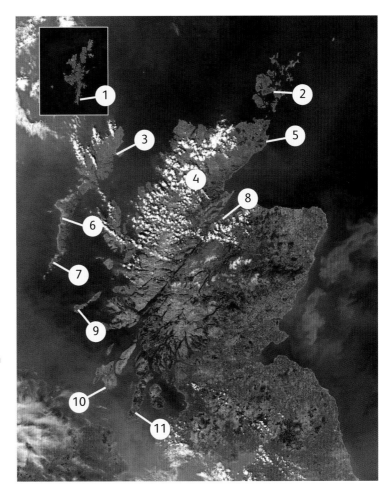

1. **Sumburgh** has regular flights to Edinburgh, Glasgow, Inverness and Aberdeen. It is the hub for much of the oil-related work in the North Sea.

2. **Kirkwall** has scheduled services to the mainland and Shetland. Other users are Fisheries Protection aircraft, Royal Mail and the Northern Lighthouse Board helicopter. Orkney has the shortest scheduled air service in the world – Westray to Papa Westray – the flight time is less than two minutes!

3. **Stornoway** gives key access to Lewis and the Western Isles with connections to Aberdeen, Inverness, Edinburgh and Glasgow. It is also an important base for the HM Coastguard search and rescue helicopter. Air-traffic control gives vital support to aircraft flying to and from North America over Iceland.

4. The largest and most frequently used Low Flying Area in the UK is the north-west Highlands.

5. **Wick** supports oil-related helicopter operations and connects to many airports in the UK.

6. **Benbecula** provides support services to the Ministry of Defence Hebrides Ranges. Connections can be made to Barra, Stornoway, Glasgow (Saab 340 aircraft) and Inverness (Jetstream 31).

7. **Barra** airport is on the north coast of the island and is washed by the tide twice a day. It is the only beach airport in the world to handle scheduled airline services. Many fly to Barra just for the experience! Flight times are subject to the tides.

8. **Inverness** is the air gateway to the Highlands and Islands. It is the largest of the 10 airports serving the region operated by Highlands and Islands airports. It handles more than 330 scheduled flights a week to Scottish and UK destinations.

9. **Tiree** is famous for surfing and often records highest annual sunshine in the UK. British Airways connects to Glasgow in Saab 340 or Twin Otter aircraft.

10. **Islay**, known as 'Queen of the Hebrides', is served by British Airways. BA connects to Glasgow in Saab 340 aircraft.

11. **Campbeltown** RAF Machrihanish was a military and NATO base until 1997. Runway (3039m) is one of the longest in Europe. Now used by British Airways and Loganair (DH6 aircraft). Able to accept the Space Shuttle if forced to land in Europe, but under threat of closure.

For information about Highlands and Islands Airports, try:
www.hial.co.uk

Making aircraft in Scotland

Scottish Aviation was an aircraft manufacturer famous for the Prestwick Pioneer and the larger Twin Pioneer ('Twin Pin').

These planes could take off and land on a very short runway. Later, Scottish Aviation built the successful Jetstream. (This plane featured in the 1979 James Bond film *Moonraker* when 007 is pushed out of the plane without a parachute!) The Bulldog training aircraft was also built there. It sold in large numbers to the Swedish Air Force, as well as to the RAF.

Scottish Aviation is now part of BAE Systems, a global company spanning five continents, and is a well-known pioneer in technology. Prestwick is still a base for aerostructures and inspires the next generation of engineers and scientists. BAE sponsors an annual Schools Aerospace Challenge.

Scotland's aerospace industry has over 150 companies. On the West Coast the aerospace corridor in Ayrshire, Lanarkshire and Renfrewshire deals with MRO – manufacture, repair and overhaul of aircraft and engines. The East Coast – Edinburgh, Fife and Tayside – works mainly in avionics, such as radar, laser systems and cockpit displays.

World-class engineering departments in the main universities ensure that genius still thrives.

A prototype of the B.125 Bulldog trainer aircraft, 1969.

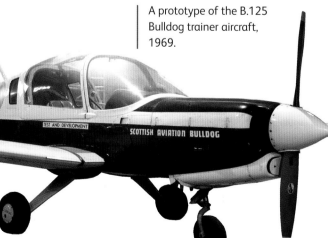

Timeline

1917
HMS *Repulse* built by John Brown's, Clydebank. The first warship with a platform fitted for aircraft to take off – the first aircraft carrier.

1913
William Beardmore & Co. had a licence to build German aeroplanes, as they built Austro-Daimler aero-engines. This was the only Scottish firm to build airships – the R34 and the engines for the R101.

1933
Engineering firm G. & J. Weir built one of the first autogyros, forerunner of the helicopter. Managing Director William Weir (1877-1959) became the first Air Minister during WWI and combined the naval and army air services into the RAF.

1935
Scottish Aviation founded at Prestwick – mainly to train pilots.

1936
Colin Campbell Mitchell of the Edinburgh firm Brown Brothers patented the slotted cylinder steam catapult. Seaplanes could now be launched at sea.

1977
Scottish Aviation became part of British Aerospace. Three years later the Jetstream was born – one of its most successful aircraft. Production ended in 1997.

1939-45
During WWII the West of Scotland employed over 30,000 people in the making of aircraft and aero-engines.

Leisure flying

The world at your feet ....

Percy Pilcher was one of the UK's earliest pioneers of heavier-than-air flight.

Percy Sinclair Pilcher (1866-99) became assistant to a Professor of Naval Architecture and Marine Engineering in Glasgow. In 1893 he began patenting small inventions and was an avid reader of anything to do with aviation. This was the year Otto Lilienthal was pioneering hang-glider flights in Germany.

Pilcher's first full-size hang glider, the *Bat*, was made in 1895, in flat-pack units ready to assemble on site. Before testing the *Bat*, Pilcher visited Lilienthal in Berlin, who advised on design changes. Further

models were designed and improved (his *Hawk* glider is in the collections of the National Museums Scotland).

Tragically, Pilcher died in a flying accident in 1899. He gave his life to the quest for flight, and a memorial to his achievements on the site of the accident reads *Icaro Alteri* – 'Another Icarus'.

Above: Percy Pilcher carrying his *Bat* 2 glider.

Right: Percy Pilcher, 1895.

Below: Pilcher in his *Hawk* glider, with his sister and helper holding on.

From Pilcher's legacy and that of many other brave aviation pioneers we can now choose all sorts of leisure flying and use the power of the wind just for fun. Gliding, hang-gliding, hot-air ballooning, kite-surfing, micro-lighting, paragliding, power-kiting and sky-diving are all looking for fellow fanatics.

Website watch

www.adventure.visitscotland.com

This site will tell you more about each sport mentioned above. Don't worry if you are not old enough to take part in these activities – it's always fun to watch!

The Scottish Flyer

The Scottish Flying Club's monthly magazine might have been eagerly read by members of the club, formed in 1927 by a few keen First World War pilots.

Cameron Balloons

Donald Allan Cameron was born in Glasgow in 1939 and became an aeronautical engineer, later joining the Bristol Aeroplane Company. His hobby of hot-air ballooning grew into a business and today Cameron Balloons in Bristol is the world's largest maker.

Cameron was the first person to cross the Sahara and the Alps by hot-air balloon. In 1999 the *Breitling Orbiter* III, built by Cameron Balloons, was the first balloon to fly non-stop around the globe.

In 2002 Steve Fossett shattered the record – flying faster and solo around the world – in another Cameron balloon.

Specially shaped balloons are used for advertising. All Cameron's craft are fully certified as aircraft. They are designed by computer, sometimes in amazing shapes.

Helicopters
Workhorses of the air

The name 'autogyro' comes from the Greek word *auto* which means 'self', and the Latin word *gyro* which means 'to circle'.

Above: The Weir W-2 Autogyro was designed and built in Scotland and first flew in 1934.

Flying a helicopter is an extremely complicated business. The pilot has to think in three dimensions, and use both hands and both feet.

The helicopter as we know it today came from the autogyro, which was devised in 1919 by Juan de la Cierva (1895-1936), a Spanish aero engineer and pilot. He moved to England in 1925 and started his own company, with help from James Weir, a Scottish industrialist. In 1928 Cierva flew an 'autogyro' across the English Channel.

Helicopters are versatile aircraft. They can take off from almost anywhere. They can hover, fly backwards, forwards and sideways. Instead of fixed wings, they have a spinning rotor with long thin blades. The blades produce lift to support the helicopter in the air. The tail rotor stops the helicopter spinning round in the opposite direction to the main rotor.

Below: Weir's autogyros lined up ready for sale.

Opposite: A Royal Navy Sea King in flight.

Helicopters are used across Scotland for countless tasks ...

HM Coastguard
Maritime Rescue Co-ordination Centres in Shetland, Stornoway, Aberdeen, the Clyde and Forth. Also air-sea rescue missions.

Scottish Ambulance Service
Emergency transfer of patients from remote areas to hospital.

Agriculture
Spreading fertiliser and renewing fencing in remote areas.

Filming
Such as *Harry Potter*, *Braveheart* and many TV shows.

Deer Commission for Scotland
Operations of deer census: counting deer, deer-culling, taking in teams safely, removing deer carcasses.

Forestry Commission
Fire-fighting, seeding, timber extraction, maintenance of tracks.

RAF Kinloss
Aeronautical Rescue Co-ordination Centre, and home to the Nimrod fleet and Search and Rescue helicopters.

RAF Leuchars
Home to a RAF Mountain Rescue Unit.

RAF Lossiemouth
Also a base for a Sea King helicopter search and rescue unit.

North Sea Oil Companies
Carrying crews and supplies to off-shore platforms and drilling rigs. Aberdeen (Dyce) and Shetland (Sumburgh) are the busiest airports in the UK for helicopter traffic.

Ordnance Survey (OS)
Aerial surveys for mapping.

Royal National Lifeboat Institution
Air-sea rescue missions.

Scottish airports
Commercial passenger flight

Scottish civil airports have enjoyed huge growth in international traffic.

Since the Open Skies policy of 1990 Scots have been able to fly direct to the United States of America and elsewhere without having to change planes at either Gatwick or Heathrow. Edinburgh is the busiest of our international airports and is a transatlantic gateway. Aberdeen is also one of Europe's busiest commercial heliports, supporting the North Sea oil and gas industry.

Above: Ecstatic female fans at Prestwick Airport in March 1960, greeting Elvis Presley, who was known by his fans as the 'King of Rock 'n' Roll'.

© NEWSQUEST

For many years Glasgow Prestwick was the only Scottish airport to operate a transatlantic link. It is a popular airport for low-budget airlines and is still a refuelling point for military aircraft. (The world-famous singer Elvis Presley set foot in Scotland here when his US Army transport plane stopped to refuel in 1960 en route to Germany.) Prestwick is also the only guaranteed fog-free airport in the United Kingdom. And, along with London Stansted, it can handle 'at risk' flights – aircraft that might have a bomb on board.

Inverness Airport (INV) is the air gateway for the Highlands and Islands of Scotland.

Let's go BRITISH CALEDONIAN

Right: British Caledonian stewardesses were famous for their tartan uniforms.

AIRPORT NAME	HISTORY (WITH PASSENGER TRAFFIC IN 2007)	AIRLINE COMPANIES	DESTIN-ATIONS	THE FUTURE
GLASGOW INTERNATIONAL (GLA)	Abbotsinch began in 1932 as an overspill for the RAF base at Renfrew and became HMS Sanderling in 1943 with the Royal Navy. Abbotsinch became the main airport in 1966 after nearby Renfrew closed. Taken over by British Airports Authority in 1975.	8.73 million	50	100	30 million passengers by 2030.
EDINBURGH (EDI)	Turnhouse Aerodrome was the most northern air defence base in WWI with the Royal Flying Corps in 1915. It became RAF Turnhouse in 1918. First London shuttle in 1947. Taken over by BAA in 1971.	9.04	50	100	Another runway by 2030. Tram network will connect to city in 2011.
ABERDEEN (ABZ)	Opened at Dyce in 1934. In WWII it was used as an RAF base. Fighters were based there to give protection from German bombing raids from occupied Norway. Taken over by BAA in 1947. Helicopter operations began in 1967. Now half the traffic is helicopter based.	3.41	85	35	Extension of runway to allow direct transatlantic flights.
GLASGOW PRESTWICK (PIK)	Began in 1934 as a training airfield. In 1938 it had passenger facilities. In 1964 the extended airport was opened. United States Air Force base from 1952-66. Part of this site is now HMS Gannet with Naval Air Squadron Sea Kings.	2.42	Hub for Ryanair and other budget airlines.	30+	Plans to be ready to handle the giant Airbus A380 when it comes into operation.

The early days of Scottish Airports

Left to right: Sumburgh Aerodrome, Shetland; a plane on the beach at Barra, Western Isles, c.1946; control tower at Turnhouse, Edinburgh, 1991; Scottish airways controllers, Prestwick Airport, 1960; Prestwick switchboard section, 1960.

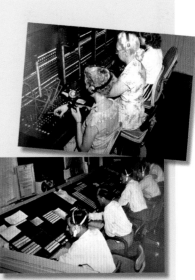

Golf Bravo Oscar Alpha Alpha
The Concorde Experience

In April 2004 the aeroplane that launched British Airways' supersonic service in 1976 came to East Fortune.

Rolls-Royce Olympus 593 engine, which provided the power for Concorde.

This was a unique challenge, as 'Alpha Alpha's' historic final journey from Heathrow Airport was made not in the air, but by land and sea! The Concorde story that enthralled the world is the centrepiece of the National Museum of Flight. Scotland beat 60 other bids to get the plane. Now visitors, young and old, enjoy the interactive exhibition and audio tour – as told by Captain Jock Reid, a Scottish Concorde pilot.

No visit is complete until all the museum outbuildings and hangars are explored. If you are making a winter visit to East Fortune, wrap up warmly to view the historic aircraft that tell the story of flight. The museum oozes with aviation history.

 Website watch
www.nms.ac.uk

Check out the National Museums Scotland website for special events at the National Museum of Flight.

Detailed directions are provided to help you find the museum, located 20 miles east of Edinburgh, off the B1347.

Concorde facts

- Only 20 Concordes were ever built. G-BOAA first flew in 1976. After the fatal Concorde accident in Paris on 25 July 2000, G-BOAA made its final flight from JFK Airport, New York to London Heathrow on 12 August 2000.

- Concorde flew higher than any other plane at 60,000 feet, close to the edge of the stratosphere, where the curvature of the Earth could be seen from the plane's windows.

- Concorde required specialist handling and was only operated by experienced pilots. Cabin crew were limited to a three-year period to maintain service standards.

- On take-off half its weight was fuel. It only managed 17 miles per gallon per passenger, much less efficient than conventional passenger aircraft.

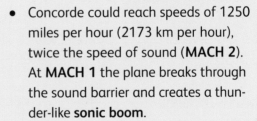

- Concorde could reach speeds of 1250 miles per hour (2173 km per hour), twice the speed of sound (**MACH 2**). At **MACH 1** the plane breaks through the sound barrier and creates a thunder-like **sonic boom**.

- Concorde was streamlined with slender delta or D-shaped wings designed to reduce drag.

- Gold-plated windows reduced the sun's harmful rays.

The flight deck of Concorde.

Future flight
Scotland 2040

From supersonic to hypersonic may be the future! Rockets travel at speeds of 5 to 10 times the speed of sound to go into orbit.

It could be that Scotland will have its own space port. Space tourism would have commercial passenger flights into space. Craft are now being developed for suborbital flight, at heights of up to 160 kilometres. Even space hotels are being planned. By 2040 there could well be resorts and holidays on the Moon ....

Space shuttle *Columbia* on the launch pad before the first mission, 12 April 1981.

But for the more earthbound, your own flat-pack plane could be the answer. Old World War airfields might yet be pressed back into service. Seaplanes could access cities or towns with inland waterways, and solar-powered lightweight flying machines might replace snarled-up road traffic.

Who can foretell the future of flight? You might be the next genius to defy gravity and greenhouse gases by 2040. Now that you have read this book, you are off to a flying start ... the sky's the limit!

Background: The Arctic plain of Mars.

Right: NASA astronaut Alan Shepard, the first American in space.

Gemini

The spacecraft below is a NASA (National Air and Space Administration) space capsule. The capsule was part of the USA's Gemini missions to send astronauts into space in the 1960s. It was designed to land in the desert instead of the ocean.

Right: The far side of the Moon, seen for the first time by Apollo 8. The Moon has a 'farside', as it rotates at the same speed it revolves around the Earth, so keeping the same face towards Earth. This means that we on Earth never get to see this side, as it is constantly facing out into the Solar system.

Background: Astronaut Bruce McCandless flies free of the space shuttle in 1984 using a jet-pack propelled by nitrogen. He managed to get 320 feet away from the shuttle.

Fast fact

Every year the Careers Scotland Festival of Science and Enterprise arranges visits to Scottish schools by NASA astronauts and scientists. Some school-children are lucky to be chosen to visit the NASA Spacecentre.

Did you know?

Alan Bean the Apollo astronaut is said to have taken a piece of specially woven MacBean tartan to the Moon in November 1969. What might you take on a journey to the Moon?

Another astronaut, Colonel Jerry Ross, took these samples of Ross tartans with him in space shuttle *Atlantis* in 1995.

And finally ... UFOs
The Bonnybridge Triangle

Scotland has had more sightings of Unidentified Flying Objects per head of population than anywhere else in the world.

Bonnybridge is in the 'Falkirk Triangle', the scene of around 300 UFO sightings every year. Ron Halliday, a local writer on UFOs, calls it 'a kind of window into another dimension'. The Scottish tourist organisation Visit Scotland tries to lure visitors to the Bonnybridge area by calling it the 'Costa del Sol for aliens'!

Twenty-five years ago Bob Taylor, a forestry worker, walked into a large clearing and saw a circular object. Two more spheres came out of it and rolled towards him. He passed out and woke up about 20 minutes later feeling terrible. Police were completely baffled by the event.

In 1997 a black triangular UFO was seen hovering above the M9 motorway by car passengers near Stirling. The object had a small rectangular bar at one apex. The sides of the triangle were judged to be between 30 and 40 feet in length.

Quick question

Name the other famous 'triangle', scene of countless mysterious events?

Answer on page 39

West Kilbride has been confirmed by the Ministry of Defence as another UFO hotspot. Sightings have been consistent – yellow spheres, sometimes alone, sometimes flying in groups of up to 25, hovering over the hills around West Kilbride.

According to experts at the Defence Intelligence Staff who have studied the reports, it is gas clouds that are glowing. Airflow changes their shape until they look like small airships speeding through the sky. Officially the MOD said in 2000 that the phenomena are not hostile! Yet they are still shrouded in mystery.

International UFO Day

An International UFO Day is held on 2 July every year. Perhaps you might like to join the skywatch and look out for strange happenings in the sky!

ANSWERS

Page 2: **Quick question** – the parts of the world not known
to people who lived in Europe 500 years ago include:
Antarctica, the west coast of America, Australasia.

Page 24: **Quick questions** – unique features include:
(a) Tiree – which has the highest annual level of sunshine in Scotland.
(b) Campbeltown – which has the longest runway in Europe.
(c) Barra – which has the only beach airport in the world; and Orkney – which has the shortest scheduled air service in the world.

Page 38: **Quick question** – the Bermuda Triangle.

Activity section, page viii:
Word search – the answers.

C	O	A	S	T	G	U	A	R	D	F	D	V	B
P	I	X	I	M	O	N	T	R	O	S	E	J	I
R	T	H	S	A	M	U	E	T	G	J	H	W	S
E	I	A	T	O	F	D	T	B	F	I	I	S	K
S	P	I	T	F	I	R	E	A	I	N	E	A	Y
T	K	B	H	L	M	O	O	L	G	O	E	W	A
W	C	A	G	H	E	Z	P	L	H	X	S	S	W
I	O	R	K	K	P	I	L	O	T	A	U	E	N
C	C	T	J	J	Y	N	A	O	H	I	O	A	U
K	J	E	F	X	U	G	N	N	B	R	H	P	R
Y	J	E	T	S	T	R	E	A	M	S	N	L	A
M	E	L	S	A	R	O	S	Y	T	H	R	A	D
L	E	U	C	H	A	R	S	K	L	I	U	N	A
R	A	F	K	H	E	L	I	C	O	P	T	E	R

PLACES OF INTEREST

Please check opening times carefully before visiting.

NATIONAL MUSEUMS SCOTLAND:
www.nms.ac.uk

NATIONAL MUSEUM OF FLIGHT
East Fortune Airfield, East Lothian EH39 5LF
Tel. 0131-247-4238

NATIONAL MUSEUM OF SCOTLAND
Chambers Street, Edinburgh EH1 1JF
Tel. 0131-225-7534

NATIONAL WAR MUSEUM
Edinburgh Castle, Edinburgh EH1 2NG
Tel. 0131-247-4413

DUMFRIES & GALLOWAY AVIATION MUSEUM
Former Control Tower, Heathhall Industrial Estate,
Heathhall, Dumfries DG7 3PH
Tel. 01387-251623
www.dumfriesaviationmuseum.com

GLASGOW SCIENCE CENTRE
50 Pacific Quay, Glasgow G51 1EA
Tel. 0871-540-1000
(Look out for their workshops in the press.)
www.glasgowsciencecentre.org

HIGHLAND AVIATION MUSEUM
9 Dalcross Industrial Estate, Inverness IV2 7XB
Tel. 01667-461100

KELVINGROVE ART GALLERY & MUSEUM
Argyle Street, Glasgow G3 8AG
Tel. 0141-276-9599
www.glasgowmuseums.com

MONTROSE AIR STATION HERITAGE CENTRE
Waldron Road, Broomfield, Montrose, DD10 9BB
Tel. 01674-678222
www.rafmontrose.org.uk

SCOTLAND'S SECRET BUNKER
Scotcrown Limited, Crown Buildings, Troywood,
near St Andrews, Fife KY16 8QH
Tel. 01333-310301
www.secretbunker.co.uk

USEFUL WEBSITES

BAA (British Airports Authority)
www.baa.com/education
– Visit 'Jumbo & Jet' with interactive games all about airports.
– 'DataPort' is for older readers, where you can explore an exciting virtual airport environment.

BBC www.bbc.co.uk/scotlandonfilm

Highlands and Islands Airports
www.hial.co.uk

Hindenburg
www.vidicom-tv.com/hindenburg

NASA www.nasa.gov/audience/
forkids/kidsclub/flash/index.html
– for NASA Kids Club.

USEFUL WEBSITES (cont'd)

National Museums Scotland
>**www.nms.ac.uk/kidsonly.aspx**
>– Visit 'Kids only' to build your own plane.

Visit Scotland
>**www.adventure.visitscotland.com**
>– For a glimpse of adventurous activities in Scotland.

Wikipedia
>**www.wikipedia.org**
>– The free online encyclopaedia.

WW2 in the Highlands and Islands of Scotland
>**www.ww2inthehighlands.co.uk**

FURTHER CREDITS

THE CONCORDE EXPERIENCE (Edinburgh: NMS Enterprises Limited – Publishing, 2005).

EAST FORTUNE TO NEW YORK – JULY 1919 (National Museums Scotland, 1979).

THE FIRST BALLOON FLIGHTS IN GREAT BRITAIN (C. L. Thompson) (National Museums Scotland, 1984).

A HISTORY OF EAST FORTUNE AERODROME (G. Newman) (National Museums Scotland, n.d.).

HOW DOES IT FLY? (National Museums Scotland, n.d.) – for illustrations in Art Section, pages iv-v.

KAY'S PORTRAITS (Edinburgh, 1842).

LANDMARKS IN THE HISTORY OF FLIGHT (National Museums Scotland, n.d.) – for illustrations in Art Section, pages ii-iii, viii.

NATIONAL MUSEUM OF FLIGHT: A Brief History of East Fortune and a Guide to the Hangers (G. Newman, P. Hazlewood, G. Cheeseman and J. Ericsson) (Edinburgh: NMS Enterprises Limited – Publishing, 2008).

R34: TWICE ACROSS THE ATLANTIC (I. T. Bunyan) (National Museums Scotland, 1989).

BRITISH AIRWAYS
(© British Airways, photographer John M. Dibbs/The Plane Picture Company) – for page 35 (Concorde over clouds).

THE BRITISH MUSEUM
(© The Trustees of the British Museum) – for page 4 (Tytler ticket).

freephotos.org
(© copyright-free-photos.org.uk) – for page 19 (jackdaw).

FRANCES AND GORDON JARVIE
for page 7 (memorial plaque).

THE LIBRARY OF CONGRESS (Prints and Photographs Division, Washington DC 20540, USA) – for pages 2 (Icarus); 3 (Stirling Castle, 1890-1900); 5 (Montgolfiers' balloon).

LOCH LOMOND SEAPLANES
(© Loch Lomond Seaplanes) – for page 21 (Cessna).

It's child's-play at the National Museum of Flight at East Fortune, East Lothian.

NASA
(© NASA Aeronautics and Space Administration) – for pages 24, 25 (aerial map of Scotland); 36 (Columbia, Alan Shepard, Arctic Plain on Mars); 37 ('farside', Bruce McCandless); 38 (space background).

NEWSQUEST
(© Image courtesy of The Herald & Evening Times picture archive) – for page 32 (Elvis Presley).

PERTHSHIRE PICTURE AGENCY
(© Graeme Hart/Perthshire Picture Agency) – for page 31 (RN Sea King Helicopter).

PHILIP JARRETT
– for page 28 (three images of Percy Pilcher), taken from *PERCY PILCHER AND THE CHALLENGE OF FLIGHT* (Edinburgh: NMSE–Publishing, 2001).

NATIONAL LIBRARY OF SCOTLAND
(© Sir Frances Ogilvy and the Trustees of the National Library of Scotland) – for page 2 (James IV and Queen Margaret).

TAIN & DISTRICT MUSEUM
(© Tain & District Museum) – for page 37 (Tartan taken to the moon).

BOB THOMPSON
(© Bob Thompson) – for page 18 (Avro Lancaster).

THE TIMES
(© NI Syndication) – for page 15 (flight over Everest).

Flight in Scotland
Facts and activities

This book belongs to:

_____

Write your name on the above line.

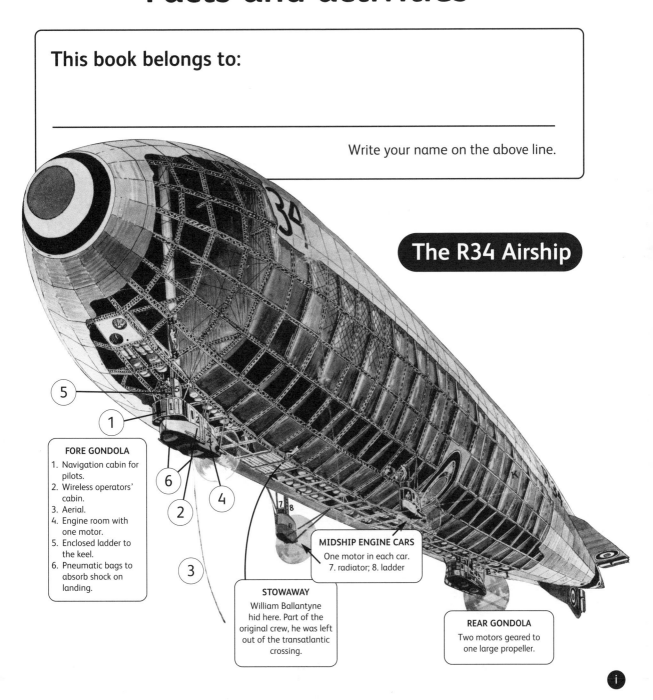

The R34 Airship

5

1

FORE GONDOLA
1. Navigation cabin for pilots.
2. Wireless operators' cabin.
3. Aerial.
4. Engine room with one motor.
5. Enclosed ladder to the keel.
6. Pneumatic bags to absorb shock on landing.

6

2

4

3

STOWAWAY
William Ballantyne hid here. Part of the original crew, he was left out of the transatlantic crossing.

MIDSHIP ENGINE CARS
One motor in each car.
7. radiator; 8. ladder

REAR GONDOLA
Two motors geared to one large propeller.

World of Flight timeline

18th century

1783   The Montgolfier brothers took to the skies in their hot-air balloon for the first aerial voyage.

19th century

1853   A glider flew, designed by Sir George Cayley and carrying a man.

1891   Otto Lilienthal from Germany made the first controlled *gliding* flights.

20th century

1903   The Wright brothers, Orville and Wilbur, made the first *powered* flight on 17 December 1903 at Kitty Hawk, North Carolina, USA. They flew 852 feet (260 metres).

1909   Louis Blériot took off from Baraques, near Calais, in a monoplane, and flew over the English Channel, arriving at Dover 37 minutes later.

1914-18 During World War I aeroplanes were used as military machines.

1919   A Vickers Vimy bomber flown by John Alcock and Arthur Whitten Brown made the first non-stop transatlantic crossing. The R34 airship completed a transatlantic crossing two weeks later.

1919   The world's first commercial and scheduled air service began.

1923   Juan de la Cierva's Autogyro flew for the first time.

1925   The de Havilland Moth first flew, starting a worldwide flying movement.

late 1920s and '30s Flying boats helped to open up overseas airline routes.

The biggest aircraft by 1929 was the Dornier DO X flying boat.

The first air hostess was hired. Ellen Church, a trained nurse and pilot, worked on the Chicago to San Francisco Boeing Air Transport route.

1933 The first modern-type airliner flew (Boeing 247).

1939 The first turbo-jet aeroplane flew (Heinkel He 178) from Rostock, Germany on 27 August.

1939-42 Jet design played an important part in World War II. And Igor Sikorsky developed the modern type of helicopter (VS-300).

1942 German A4 rocket took off and the Space Age began.

1947 Bell X-1 broke the sound barrier.

1952 The de Havilland Comet began the first jet airliner passenger service.

1954 The first jet vertical take-off was achieved – the 'Flying Bedstead'.

1959 The first hovercraft (SRN-1) 'flew' across the English Channel.

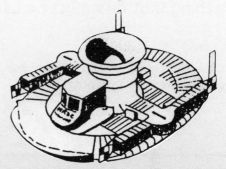

1969 On 20 July Neil Armstrong and Edwin 'Buzz' Aldrin stepped onto the surface of the Moon.

1969 Concorde's maiden flight.

1970 Boeing's wide-bodied 747, the first 'jumbo jet', carries 500 passengers.

1976 Concorde began the first supersonic jet airliner service, carrying 100 passengers at twice the speed of sound.

1981 The first flight of the Space Shuttle.

1988 The first airliner with computers that could pilot the plane went into service – the A320 Airbus.

21st century

2008 The first civilian pays to join a flight into space …

How does it fly?
Forces of nature

Anything that flies must be LIGHT.

Let's begin with Birds …

Birds have hollow, air-filled bones and a body-covering of feathers ('light as a feather').

Bats …

their wings have a framework of long slender bones with a covering of paper-thin skin.

Flying insects …

have paper-thin wings and stiff, but light, bodies.

Forces

There are four forces which work on an aeroplane or flying animal.

1 **Lift** and **weight** works to make it go up.

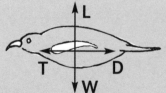

2 **Gravity** acts to make it fall down.

3 **Thrust** works to make it move forwards.

4 **Drag** works to slow it down.

Model aeroplanes …

are made of paper, balsa wood or light plastic.

Real aeroplanes …

today are built of light metals, mainly aluminium alloys, but in the past planes would have been made of wood, and even paper and light fabrics were used in construction. All these materials are **LIGHT**.

Colour in the pictures on this page, or any of the pages of this section.

It must have LIFT and WEIGHT ...

But no matter how light they are, flying animals and aeroplanes are pulled downwards by the **force of gravity** (their **weight**); so their wings are used to provide **lift**. An aeroplane's lift is mostly due to the shape of its wings. If you cut through the wing you'll see that it is quite thick at the front (leading edge) and tapers away

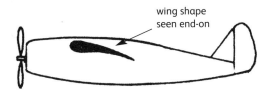

wing shape seen end-on

towards the back (trailing edge). This is the shape of an airfoil: a curved top surface and a flatter bottom one. The airfoil makes heavier-than-air flight possible.

> The shape of the wing means that both the upper surface and the lower surface cause the air that passes over them to be forced down. We know that 'to every action there is an equal and opposite reaction' (from Isaac Newton's Third Law of Motion), which means that if you push something one way there is an equal force in the opposite direction – hence the air is forced down and the aeroplane up.

... and THRUST and DRAG

Anything that flies must have something to move it forwards through the air: something to provide **thrust**. This usually comes from the engine of the aircraft, or the muscles of the animal. **Thrust** has to work against **drag**, the slowing-down action (**wind resistance**) of the air rubbing against the skin of the aircraft or animal. To cut down on **drag**, flying objects are streamlined.

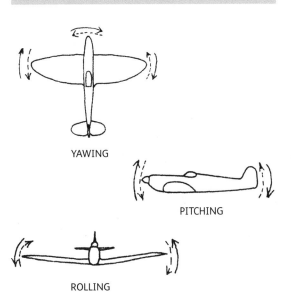

YAWING

PITCHING

ROLLING

... and CONTROL.

As air is never still and gusts of wind may blow an aeroplane about and disturb its level flight, the pilot must control these disturbances.

By using moveable surfaces on the wings and tail, a pilot can make the plane **yaw**, **pitch** or **roll** to change directions, or to

control any disturbance. He can push the **rudder bar** with his feet, right or left, and the nose will swing in his chosen direction.

A **control stick** in front of the seat will raise or lower **elevator panels** on the tail which in turn lowers or raises the nose.

Each wing has an **aileron**, a surface that can move up or down. The control stick can be moved left or right, the chosen aileron goes up and the plane will **roll** (or bank) in the required direction.

R34's journey

From 2 to 13 July 1919 the R34 airship completed an epic two-way transatlantic crossing. The route went from East Fortune Airfield in East Lothian, to Mineola near New York, then back over the Atlantic to land eventually in Pulham in Norfolk.

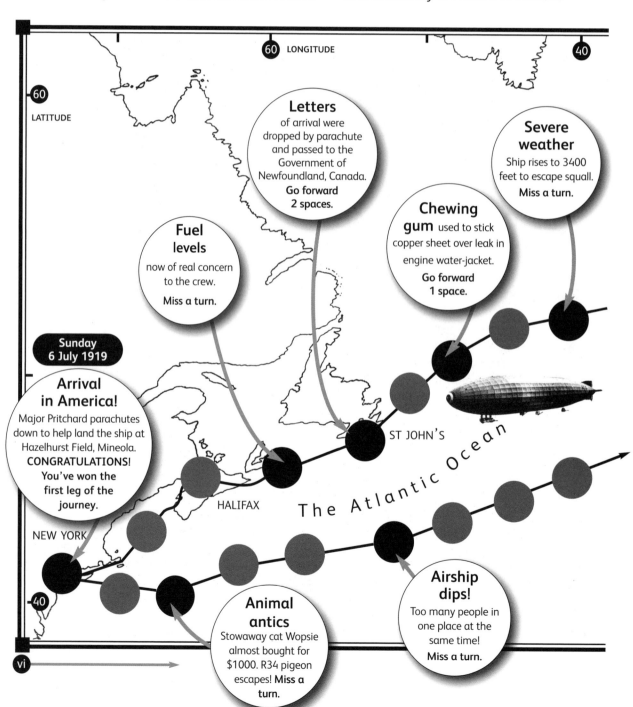

60 LONGITUDE

40

60
LATITUDE

Letters
of arrival were dropped by parachute and passed to the Government of Newfoundland, Canada.
Go forward 2 spaces.

Severe weather
Ship rises to 3400 feet to escape squall.
Miss a turn.

Chewing gum used to stick copper sheet over leak in engine water-jacket.
Go forward 1 space.

Fuel levels
now of real concern to the crew.
Miss a turn.

Sunday 6 July 1919

Arrival in America!
Major Pritchard parachutes down to help land the ship at Hazelhurst Field, Mineola.
CONGRATULATIONS!
You've won the first leg of the journey.

ST JOHN'S

The Atlantic Ocean

HALIFAX

NEW YORK

40

Animal antics
Stowaway cat Wopsie almost bought for $1000. R34 pigeon escapes! **Miss a turn.**

Airship dips!
Too many people in one place at the same time!
Miss a turn.

vi

This is a game for 2 players. You will need a coin. You will also need a small counter for each player. Follow the instructions on the dots you land on.

To move, toss the coin:
Heads = move counter 2 spaces; **Tails** = move 1 space
The winner is the player who 'flies' to America and back first!

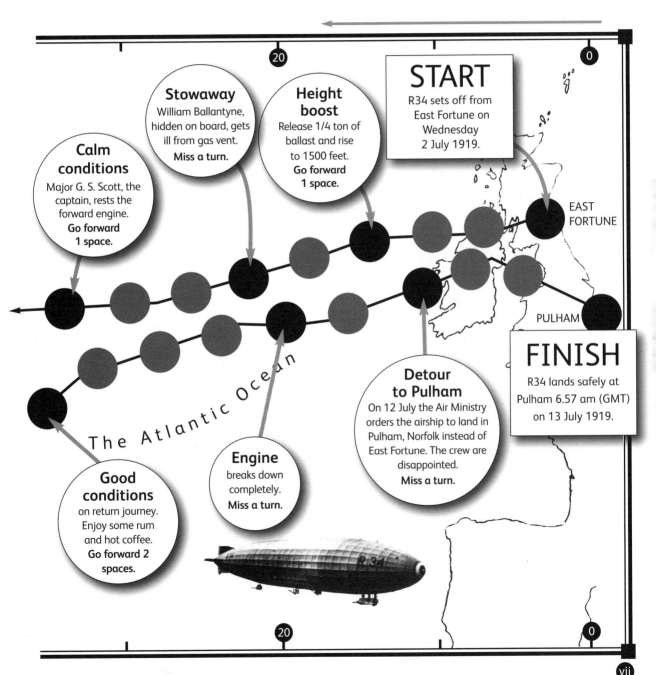

START
R34 sets off from East Fortune on Wednesday 2 July 1919.

Height boost
Release 1/4 ton of ballast and rise to 1500 feet.
Go forward 1 space.

Stowaway
William Ballantyne, hidden on board, gets ill from gas vent.
Miss a turn.

Calm conditions
Major G. S. Scott, the captain, rests the forward engine.
Go forward 1 space.

EAST FORTUNE

PULHAM

FINISH
R34 lands safely at Pulham 6.57 am (GMT) on 13 July 1919.

Detour to Pulham
On 12 July the Air Ministry orders the airship to land in Pulham, Norfolk instead of East Fortune. The crew are disappointed.
Miss a turn.

Engine breaks down completely.
Miss a turn.

Good conditions
on return journey. Enjoy some rum and hot coffee.
Go forward 2 spaces.

The Atlantic Ocean

R34

20

0

Flight fun

Word search

There are 28 words about flying on airplanes, airports and flight in Scotland hidden in this word square. Can you find them? You can move diagonally, as well as up and down, in any direction, to find the words listed below:

Answers on page 39

C	O	A	S	T	G	U	A	R	D	F	D	T	B
P	I	X	I	M	O	N	T	R	O	S	E	J	I
R	T	H	S	A	M	U	E	T	G	J	H	W	S
E	I	A	T	O	F	D	T	B	F	I	I	S	K
S	P	I	T	F	I	R	E	A	I	N	E	A	Y
T	K	B	H	L	M	O	O	L	G	O	E	W	A
W	C	A	G	H	E	Z	P	L	H	X	S	S	W
I	O	F	I	K	P	I	L	O	T	A	U	E	N
C	C	T	L	J	T	N	A	O	H	I	O	A	U
K	J	E	F	Y	U	G	N	N	B	R	H	P	R
L	J	E	T	S	T	R	E	A	M	S	N	L	A
M	E	L	S	A	R	O	S	Y	T	H	R	A	D
L	E	U	C	H	A	R	S	K	L	I	U	N	A
R	A	F	F	H	E	L	I	C	O	P	T	E	R

AIR	HELICOPTER	ROSYTH
AIRSHIP	JET	RUNWAY
BALLOON	JETSTREAM	SEAPLANE
COCKPIT	LEUCHARS	SKY
COASTGUARD	MONTROSE	SPITFIRE
DOGFIGHT	PILOT	TURNHOUSE
FLIGHT	PLANES	TYTLER
FLY	PRESTWICK	WING
FUEL	RADAR	
GLIDER	RAF	

Golf Bravo Oscar Alpha Alpha

Concorde GBOAA used the international radio operator code to identify itself. Think of a call sign (your aircraft registration) – or use your own name. Then use the radio alphabet below to identify yourself.

The NATO Alphabet was designed so that voice messages can be clearly understood. English must be used for communication between an aircraft and a control tower whenever two nations are involved.

Alpha	**N**ovember
Bravo	**O**scar
Charlie	**P**apa
Delta	**Q**uebec
Echo	**R**omeo
Foxtrot	**S**ierra
Golf	**T**ango
Hotel	**U**niform
India	**V**ictor
Juliet	**W**hisky
Kilo	**X**-ray
Lima	**Y**ankee
Mike	**Z**ulu